WHAT'S GNU?

Riddles from the Zoo

by Thomas Mase
pictures by Susan Slattery Burke

Lerner Publications Company · Minneapolis

*To the notion that there are no bad puns, only people
who don't appreciate good word play   —T.M.*

*To my brother, Pat, for his sunny voice on the phone
every morning   —S.S.B*

Copyright © 1990 by Lerner Publications Company

This book is available in two editions:
Library binding by Lerner Publications Company
Soft cover by First Avenue Editions
241 First Avenue North
Minneapolis, Minnesota 55401

Library of Congress Cataloging-in-Publication Data

Mase, Thomas
    What's gnu?:riddles from the zoo/by Thomas Mase; pictures by Susan
Slattery Burke.
        p.   cm.—(You must be joking)
    Summary: A collection of animal riddles, including "What do tortoises wear
to keep warm? Turtleneck sweaters."
    ISBN 0-8225-2330-2 (lib. bdg.)
    ISBN 0-8225-9581-8 (pbk.)
    1. Riddles, Juvenile. 2. Animals—Juvenile humor. [1. Riddles. 2. Animals—Wit
and humor.] I. Burke, Susan Slattery, ill. II. Title. III. Series.
PN6371.5.M37   1990
818'.5402—dc20   89-36627
                                                            CIP
                                                            AC

Manufactured in the United States of America

    2 3 4 5 6 7 8 9 10 99 98 97 96 95 94 93 92 91

Q: What is a camel's favorite snack food?

A: Camelcorn.

Q: How do the wild dogs of Africa celebrate Halloween?

A: By carrying jackal lanterns.

Q: What is the favorite food of the South American llama?

A: Llama beans.

Q: What did the dolphin say when his trainer accused him of ruining the show?

A: "I didn't do it on porpoise."

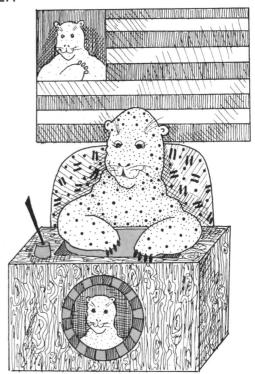

Q: Which sea lion has a permanent home in the White House?

A: The Presidential Seal.

Q: What do porpoises have on New Year's Eve?
A: A whale of a party.

Q: Which insects are whizzes at math?
A: The arithmetick and the inchworm.

Q: What do you have when two ants run away to get married?
A: An ant-elope.

Q: Why did the doctor hesitate to tell the bee he might have hives?
A: She didn't want to make a rash decision.

Q: What was the centipede's biggest complaint after running a marathon?
A: The agony of defeet.

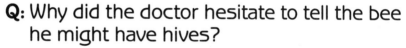

Q: What do you call a sea bird who is easily fooled?

A: Gull-ible.

Q: What fish gives other fish a black eye?

A: The sockeye salmon.

Q: What happens when shellfish exercise too much?

A: They become musselbound.

Q: Why do fish travel in schools?
A: To show they have a lot of class.

Q: What do you get when you cross a homing dove with a small dog?

A: A terrier pigeon.

Q: Has any bird ever served as pope?

A: No, but many of them are cardinals.

Q: What bird belongs in an insane asylum?

A: A loon-atic.

Q: What do you call a crow who talks wildly and irrationally?

A: A raven idiot.

Q: Where do most condors make their nests?
A: In condor-miniums.

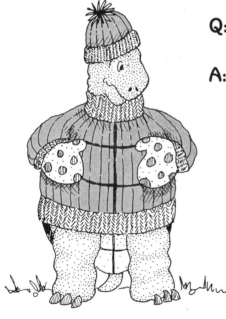

Q: What do you get when you cross an ostrich with a blue-winged duck?

A: A really big teal.

Q: What amphibian has become part of everyone's address?

A: The ZIP toad.

Q: How do tortoises keep warm?

A: They wear turtleneck sweaters.

Q: What snake is an important part of every automobile?

A: The windshield viper.

Q: If you spotted a large reptile in a passageway between buildings, what would it probably be?

A: An alley-gator.

Q: Have crocodiles learned to cook in microwave ovens?

A: No. They're still using croc pots.

Q: How does the king of beasts prefer to catch his dinner?

A: By lion in wait.

Q: What did the scientist say when she discovered a wildcat thought to be extinct?

A: "I've found the missing lynx!"

Q: Which cats were expelled from school because they had stolen the answers to the final exam?

A: The cheatahs.

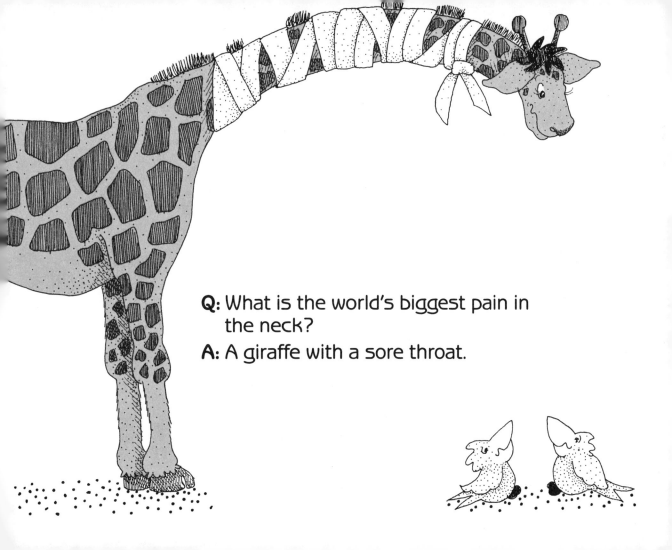

Q: What is the world's biggest pain in the neck?

A: A giraffe with a sore throat.

Q: What do you call someone who sells goods to female deer?

A: A doe-to-doe salesperson.

Q: What would you use to give a hippopotamus a flu shot?

A: A hippo-dermic needle.

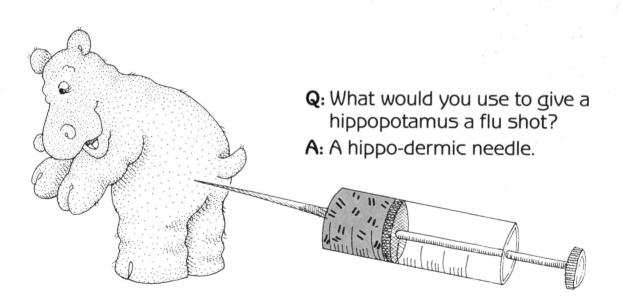

Q: What do you call a young deer who trims the grass?

A: A fawn mower.

Q: What would you call a country populated only by male deer?

A: Stag nation.

Q: Why did the teacher put the deer in the corner?

A: He was moose-behaving.

Q: When the fox family was dining on shore birds, what did the mother tell her hungry son?

A: "Wait for your tern."

Q: Do grizzlies ever wear caps?

A: No. They always go bear-headed.

Q: Why would pandas have been good actors in silent movies?

A: They excel at pandamime.

Q: What item that most tourists carry was invented by a bear?

A: The Kodiak camera.

Q: What do you have when grizzlies fall into a vat of glue?
A: Gummy bears.

Q: Why are gnus afraid of catching colds?

A: They're worried they might develop gnumonia.

Q: How do Tibetan oxen act when they see a funny movie?

A: They really yak it up.

Q: What is a buffalo's favorite dessert?
A: Bisonberry pie.

Q: Do oxen wear sneakers?
A: No. Only oxfords.

: What do you call a male sheep who knocks down doors?

A: A battering ram.

Q: What do you call a female horse who is awake from dusk to dawn?

A: A night mare.

Q: Where do you take a stallion when he's sick?

A: To the horsepital.

Q: Where do young cows eat their lunch at school?

A: In the calf-eteria.

Q: What would you call a herd of cows motoring down the highway?

A: Cattle drivers.

Q: Why is it hard to understand what turkeys say?

A: All they speak is gobbledygook.

Q: How do roosters sign their names?

A: With a ball-point hen.

Q: Would you tell a secret to a pig?

A: No. He'd probably squeal.

Q: Do rabbits enjoy horror movies?
A: No. They're too hare-raising.

Q: How do hares travel in large cities?
A: By rabbit transit.

Q: Do pigs make good drivers?
A: No. They're road hogs.

Q: Why did a fast-food chain open a restaurant for primates?

A: They were hoping for a lot of monkey business.

Q: Do gorillas like orange juice?

A: No. They only like apefruit juice.

Q: What is a gorilla's favorite dessert?

A: Chocolate chimp cookies.

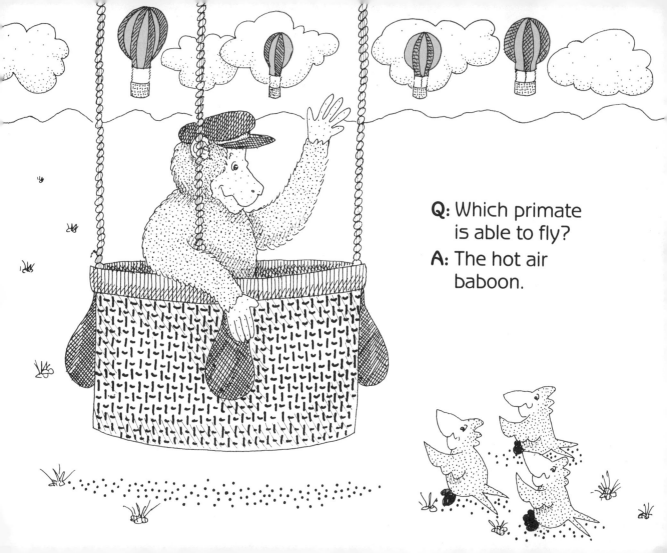

Q: Which primate is able to fly?

A: The hot air baboon.

Q: What do primate youngsters love to play on in the schoolyard?

A: The monkey bars.

Q: If a monkey is like his father, what is he often called?

A: A chimp off the old block.

Q: What are monkeys' favorite flowers?

A: Chimp pansies.

Q: When the gorilla got a pain in her stomach, what did the doctors call it?

A: Ape-pendicitis.

Q: Where do chimpanzees get most of their news?
A: They hear it through the apevine.

ABOUT THE AUTHOR

Thomas Mase lives in Rhinelander, Wisconsin. A graduate of the University of Wisconsin, Tom was a newspaper reporter, a wire editor, and a junior high school English teacher. Now a freelance writer, he enjoys creating and solving puzzles and word games. He loves to play cards.

ABOUT THE ARTIST

Susan Slattery Burke loves to illustrate fun-loving characters, especially animals. To her, each of them has a personality all their own. Her satisfaction comes when the characters come to life for the reader. Susan lives in Minneapolis, Minnesota, with her husband, her dog, and her cat. She is a graduate of the University of Minnesota. Susan enjoys sculpting, travel, illustrating, entertaining, and being outdoors.

You Must Be Joking

Alphabatty: Riddles from A to Z
Help Wanted: Riddles about Jobs
Here's to Ewe: Riddles about Sheep
Hide and Shriek: Riddles about Ghosts and Goblins
Ho Ho Ho! Riddles about Santa Claus
I Toad You So: Riddles about Frogs and Toads
On with the Show: Show Me Riddles
Out on a Limb: Riddles about Trees and Plants
That's for Shore: Riddles from the Beach
Weather or Not: Riddles for Rain and Shine
What's Gnu? Riddles from the Zoo
Wing It! Riddles about Birds